IMAGES OF
PRESTON

IMAGES OF
PRESTON

LANCASHIRE
Evening Post

breedon **books**
PUBLISHING

First published in Great Britain by
The Breedon Books Publishing Company Limited
44 Friar Gate, Derby, DE1 1DA
1199, reprinted 2006

ISBN 1 85983 007 2

Printed and bound by Cromwell Press, Trowbridge, Wiltshire.

Contents

Foreword

PRESTON is one of the most important towns of Northern England and the photographs in this book provide reminders from earlier times of many aspects of life in this proud and historic town.

As a Prestonian the photographs remind me of the sights and sounds of my upbringing in the town and I am sure they will provide equally vivid memories for every Prestonian.

The book offers significant insights into the development of Preston as an important centre for industry and commerce, from the Industrial Revolution to more modern times.

Preston has fine civic buildings and many of historic interest, which are celebrated in the photographs.

The people of Preston are proud and warmhearted and support each other through difficult times. The photographs illustrate these characteristics and show aspects of the hardship which the proud people of Preston have had to bear.

The achievements of earlier generations and the rich and varied history of the town have not always been celebrated as they deserve and this book is a marvellous way of bringing the past alive for the current generation.

I am sure there is something of interest for everyone and I hope you enjoy looking at the photographs and reflecting on the achievements of Proud Preston.

Brian G. Booth
Vice-Chancellor
University of Central Lancashire
June 1995

Introduction

PRESTON can be proud of its claim to being one of the oldest boroughs in Britain. It can be proud, too, that historical records can trace its links with the Roman occupation of Britain and with succeeding Anglo-Saxon and Danish periods. There is little doubt that Preston's origin as a settlement was influenced by its situation on high ground overlooking the river Ribble.

It is believed the town got its name from Preosta-tun, meaning Priest-town, which is contained in a charter of Edward the Confessor's reign. Preston is mentioned in the Domesday Book of William the Conqueror and the first known religious foundation was at Tulketh where the Benedictine monks arrived in 1123. After a four-year stay they moved on to build Furness Abbey, and in 1221 the Franciscan friars arrived to give Friargate its name.

By then Preston had developed into a small but busy market town and in 1179 it had received a charter from Henry II permitting certain trading rights to the burgesses, or residents. This was known as a Guild Charter which is joyously celebrated every 20 years.

Preston has been the scene of several bloody battles — including the Scottish invasion in 1323 when Robert Bruce's soldiers set fire to the town, the Civil War in the time of Cromwell and the Jacobite Rebellions of 1715 and 1745.

Up to the Industrial Revolution, which began in the eighteenth century, the shape and size of Preston had remained virtually unchanged for hundreds of years. But with the coming of the Steam Age and the discovery of the Lancashire coalfields the face of the town began to alter rapidly.

As the population grew the patchwork of fields surrounding what was then only a market town began to be replaced by rows of terraced back-to-back houses, cobbled streets and forbidding factories.

The first water-powered cotton mill in Preston opened in 1777 in Moor Lane. In 1800, with the arrival of steam power in the town, there were 16 spinning mills operating.

By now more rural workers were abandoning the cottage crafts of handloom weaving and spinning to live and work in Preston. This resulted in many of them living in overcrowded houses and cellars within the shadow of the mills. In 1883 there were around 80 mills.

The cotton industry reached its peak around 1914, but after World War One it began to decline because of overseas competition. The last cotton mill to be built in Preston was the Embroidery Mill in 1913.

After World War Two, Preston adapted to a diversity of industries — the main one begin aircraft production which was later transferred to neighbouring Warton and Samlesbury.

Great development schemes were also undertaken after the war in Preston and many areas in the town were demolished and replaced with modern buildings and new roads.

The many photographs in this book provide a visual record of some of Preston's former places, characters and past events which are sure to interest readers of all ages.

The Changing Face

Something sensational must have happened here! This was the usual scene on Preston Market Square when General Election results were announced in the days before radio sets had become popular. The results were flashed on to the large screen from a projector on the old Town Hall steps after midnight. This photograph was taken in 1931 from the Harris Library.

This 1959 presentation by Hutton and Howick Women's Institute recaptured the spirit of the Roaring Twenties when they showed off the styles of the Flapper era.

WHY YOU SHOULD VOTE
FOR
FLORENCE WHITE

The Policy of the Government is Fixed, therefore,
A Vote for Either Party is Wasted.

BRITAIN EXPECTS –   **BRITAIN EXPECTS –**

THE ONLY ISSUE AT THIS ELECTION IS
WHETHER SPINSTERS SHALL
OR SHALL NOT HAVE JUSTICE

CITIZENS OF PRESTON
IT RESTS WITH <u>YOU</u>!

A pension for spinsters! That was the clarion call by Miss Florence White in her lone battle to win the 1936 Preston parliamentary by-election. She polled only 3,221 votes out of the 66,000 cast. The winner was the Conservative candidate Capt E.C.Cobb.

These halberds alongside the entrance of this house always marked the home of the current Mayor of Preston. The home in the picture was that of alderman Dr Derham, of Garstang Road, Preston. He was mayor of the town in 1933.

Preston Fire Brigade, 1935, in their gleaming brass Roman-style helmets and jackboots outside their fire station, then in Tithebarn Street. They were an impressive sight whenever they took part in the mayoral processions. This fire station was built in 1852 and demolished around 1967 to make way for the new bus station.

Ladies had their own tables for many years in the Harris Library's General Reading Room which had many varied newspapers and periodicals. This was soon converted to offices in the late 1960s and a much smaller reading section was allocated to the lending department.

Behind the scenes at the Harris Lending Library. All female librarians had to wear dark blue overalls with a white collar when on duty. This was relaxed after World War Two.

The Harris Library used to have a directories counter in addition to its book lending service. This picture was taken in 1935.

The Children's Library within the Harris building was a huge success when it first opened in 1935.

This building, the Preston Gas Company office and showroom in Fishergate, was demolished in 1964 to make way for the St George's Shopping Centre entrance opposite Woolworths. It was built in 1877 and then owned by a private company. It was nationalised after World War Two.

This tunnel beneath Longridge Fell was bored around 1930 to convey water from the reservoirs to Preston.

Fulwood Barracks as it looked around World War One. The barracks were built in 1847 and revamped around 1964 when the archway was removed. The royal crest, on top, now stands on the barracks front lawn.

The old Unitarian chapel, set back off Church Street, was a religious meeting house in 1716 and is one of Preston's oldest buildings. It was the town's first dissenting chapel; graves lie beneath the shrubbery.

Saul Street Methodist chapel was opened in 1837. It was bought later by the Freemasons and opened as a Masonic Temple in 1944 after which it was refronted and additions made.

Miller Arcade, built in 1901, was Preston's first élite shopping precinct. In addition to Hayhurst's Kings Arms on the corner it also had a Turkish Baths and the Geisha Dance Hall. The arcade was owned by local dentist Nathaniel Miller.

The Sir Robert Peel limestone statue in Winckley Square is still there, but the name of the Mayor of Preston who unveiled it in 1852 has been erased from the plinth (see arrow). He was Dr Thomas Monk, 61, who was jailed for life in 1857 for a minor forgery offence. Afterwards the corporation obliterated his name.

This view from the top of Cannon Street shows the Grey House and Seven Stars which fronted Fishergate. Soon after this picture was taken in 1920 it was turned into shops. The rear part of the inn was bought by George Toulmin to join part of the *Lancashire Evening Post*.

This shows the Grey House and Seven Stars from a different aspect in 1923 when it was closed down after being bought by George Toulmin's sons to extend the *Lancashire Evening Post's* premises in Fishergate. The Borough Tavern was also bought by the Toulmin family for extensions to the press-room.

St John's Place which links Church Street, alongside Preston Parish Church, down to Stoneygate was widened in 1937 and the old cottages demolished.

Handloom weavers occupied these cellared cottages once in Mount Pleasant, off Corporation Street.

Everton Gardens, off North Road, had more cobblestones than flowers. Here's how it looked in 1939. It was cleared away in the 1960s to make way for the new bus station.

This is reputed to be the oldest shop in Preston. Situated in Market Place (opposite the Flag Market) it was a tobacconists for many years until about 1964. It still remains, but not as a tobacconists.

Blackpool Road, looking west, from a point near Moor Park Serpentine. This road was only a lane until 1925 when it was widened as a circular road for Blackpool-bound traffic. It was first called the New Arterial Road.

Concreting Preston's roads and streets found work for many unemployed men during the 'Hungry Thirties'. The scene is Blackpool Road almost opposite what is now PC World.

St Vincent's Boys' Home, in Fulwood, opened in 1896, was run by the Sisters of Charity for destitute children. It was demolished in 1956 and the youngsters boarded in ordinary homes. Afterwards St Thomas More High School was built on the site and later renamed Corpus Christie High School.

The first group of children to be placed in the care of St Vincent's Home in 1896. The sisters' dress was similar to the French peasants in the area from which they were founded.

St Vincent's Boys' Band around 1920. It was renowned in the Preston area until the home closed down in 1956. The home accommodated around 300 boys.

Black Bull Lane, Fulwood, in 1937 presents a peaceful setting. This picture was taken from Queen's Drive looking south. The entrance to Fulwood Leisure Centre is now on the right, where the double telegraph poles stand. (*Photo: Harris Library*)

This caused a stir in 1950 when a driverless waggon ran backwards in London Road. No one was injured and the lamppost saved the shops, including the Troy Laundry agency next to the newsagents – all these small shops are now gone.

Gooby's will still be remembered as one of Preston's leading haberdashers in Church Street at the corner of Tithebarn Street. The shop assistants, like many other stores, had to wear black dresses when serving. Masons was known as a cut-price sweet shop and, at the extreme right, the Palladium Cinema can just be seen here in 1950.

What is now St George's Shopping Precinct used to be a maze of alleyways between Friargate and Fishergate. The chimney being dismantled was in narrow Aspinall Street, off Bambers Yard, which had several small shops.

There were once canal warehouses off Corporation Street close to the basin where the Preston end of the canal started.

The Star Cinema at the corner of Fylde Road and Corporation Street was a round-shaped building opened in 1926. It closed in 1960 and the site is now part of the university car park.

The Princes Theatre, Tithebarn Street, was first known as the Gaiety. It was later owned by Will Onda who turned it into a cinema. It closed around 1960.

The Royal Hippodrome in Friargate being demolished in 1959 to make way for C & A's store.

Pomp and ceremony as 1922 Guild Mayor alderman Astley-Bell is escorted to the Parish Church.

Umbrellas were being used by the watchers as sun-shades when this religious procession in the 1922 Guild went along Stanley Street. The bandsmen are wearing a mixture of uniforms, bowler hats, flat caps and suits.

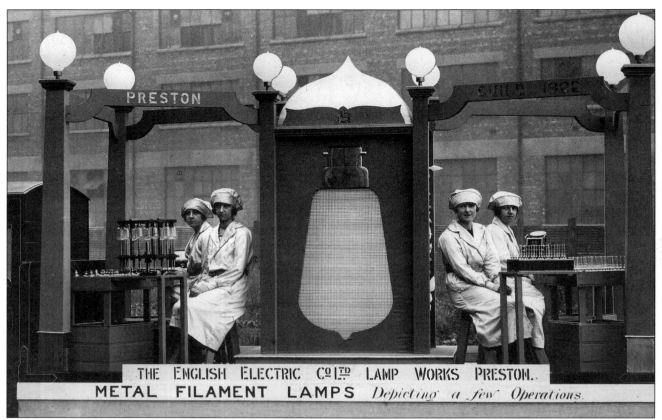

English Electric Lamp Co's 1922 Guild tableau outside the Watery Lane factory which later became Siemens Lamps.

A textile tableau passing under the bales of the cotton arch outside Horrockes HQ (left) in Stanley Street in the 1922 Guild.

Horse transport still outnumbered motor vehicle transport in the 1922 Trades procession in Church Street.

A pause in the procession. The Sunday Schools section halts in Ribbleton Lane at the corner of Deepdale Road in the 1922 Guild.

Part of the crowd at the top of London Road waiting for one of the 1922 Guild processions to pass. Cheetham Arms is on the right.

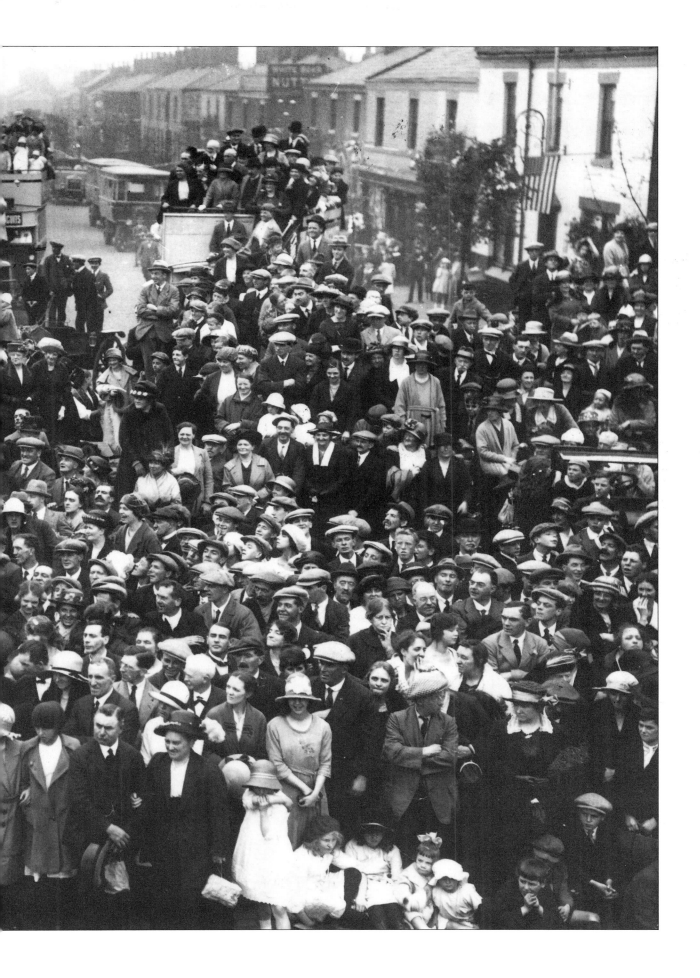

The first picture to be released in 1954 of English Electrics highly successful Canberra MK B6, details of which were then top secret.

Lord Nelson (left) presents a 40-year service award to Bill Shorrock, general manager in 1964 of English Electric, Preston. Bill started these as an apprentice at 14 and later became head of BAC and was known to many.

GEC publicity manager in 1975, Norman Gardener (left) shows an Egyptian rail chief around the Strand Road works with manager Sam Fawthorpe (right). This factory used to be part of Dick, Kerr's tram works.

Dryden's foundry in Grimshaw Street, Preston, was run by the family for three generations starting in 1871. In 1944 it was bought by Coxleys and then Deveres, but still traded as Dryden's. It closed in 1974.

Lostock Hall Gasworks as it looked in 1932 – a mere fraction of the size it was later to become. Then, when North Sea gas replaced coal gas, its size diminished again.

No, it's not Chernobyl nuclear plant ready to explode! It's Lostock Hall coal and gas works as it looked in an autumn sunset in 1970.

Clogs were the favourite footwear once for Lancashire workers – especially cotton mill operatives. Here a clog maker shapes a clog sole out of a wooden block.

A foundry worker in 1936 shaping clog irons which were sold to local cloggers.

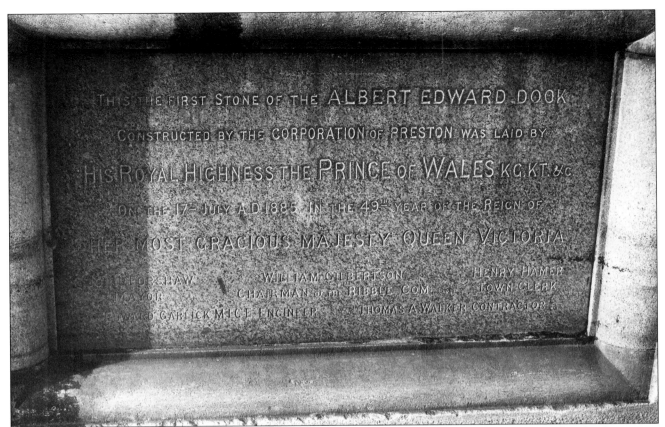

Surfaced again! Here is the actual stone in the dock wall which only became visible again after the port was closed to large ships. Throughout the years the port was open, the stone was constantly beneath the surface due to the water displacement caused by the weight of the ships.

It took three salvage attempts to raise the corporation tug *Penfold* after she sank one night in the dock in 1950. Fortunately, no one was aboard at the time. Her wheelhouse and mast are showing above the surface, The *Walter Bibby* and *Savick* were two corporation dredgers.

Preston Dock had its own diver from its earliest days. This picture was taken in 1906 and this type of diving equipment was still in use at the dock in the 1960s.

Dock diver Jack Bell entering the murky waters to try and put a cable beneath the *Penfold* in a bid to salvage her.

The tug *Penfold* moored in the Ribble after she had been salvaged. The men aboard are looking for the cause of her sinking.

A lady tramp! The most well known of all the tramp steamers to sail regularly into the dock was the *Helen Craig*. She bought her first cargo to Preston before the dock was opened and moored at a riverside wharf. She was given a momentous civic farewell and every ship in the dock gave her an emotional siren blast as she sailed for the breakers' yard in 1959. Her skipper for most of the time was captain Kennedy.

The Preston Corporation dredger *Arpley* belching out smoke on the River Ribble. Dredgers were in constant use to clear the channel of sand washed in by the tides from the Irish Sea.

Cargo ships from the USSR in 1965, moored in Preston Dock. Despite the Cold War, they often sailed into the port, but the crews were seldom allowed to go ashore. In 1962, one 21-year-old deserted and obtained political asylum in Britain.

Severe damage was caused by fire in 1964 when the Soviet ship *Igarkales* (right), bringing timber to Preston Dock, caught fire. A special tug (seen here alongside the *Igarkales*) was sent from Russia to tow the vessel home.

Here are the same stables in 1930 when they were owned by Merigold Bros as their motor car garage and showroom.

The Ribble bus station was replaced by the present bus station in 1969. The Empire Hotel can been seen left.

The old Ribble bus station as seen from the Chatham Street end.

Holidays abroad went no further than the Isle of Man for this large crowd on Preston Railway Station in 1950. The queue is for the boat-train for Fleetwood during Preston holiday week which was then held in August when the town virtually closed down.

Stand back, it's coming. This photograph appeared in the *Evening Post* on 22 July 1957, which was then the start of Preston's annual holiday week. A report in the *Post* said that, in contrast, the bus station that day had been nearly deserted, which showed that rail travel was still the most popular.

Bond Minicars made in Ribbleton, Preston, made their first appearance in 1950. A three-wheeler, it had a Villiers 125cc two-stroke engine and did up to 100 miles to a gallon of petrol. It had a roll-back canvas hood, and was the answer to European bubble cars.

The first Saul Street Baths were opened in 1851 consisting of this pool and a much smaller one. Dressing cubicles were on two floors and water often dripped through the rough wooden floorboards on to the clothes of the bathers below. Mixed bathing was forbidden. There were separate days for males and females. These baths closed in 1936.

When the old Saul Street Baths first opened, the public were allowed to use one part (seen here) to wash their clothes. In 1870 this washing service ceased, as laundries began to open elsewhere in the town

Saul Street Baths, combined with the Queen's Hall, was opened in 1936. It had two pools – one large (seen here) and one small. In its earlier years the large pool was boarded over in winter and used as a ballroom. The baths were demolished in 1991 to make way for the construction of the new Crown Court.

Haslam Park open-air baths in 1958.

Waverley Park open-air baths in Ribbleton which finally closed in 1979. This is how they looked in 1958.

Moor Park open-air baths when it closed down in 1971.

The tumbling boats were popular with the youngsters for many years at Preston's Whitsuntide Fair.

Preston's traditional Whitsuntide Fair had always lasted from Friday until Tuesday night (except for Sunday). Around 1960 the council decided to restrict the fair to Saturday and Monday because of complaints that the crowds caused traffic problems.

Whitsun Fair, May 1947, was also missing the sunshine it seems. Not that these youngsters cared.

Boxing booths and freak shows used to be part of the attractions of the Whitsuntide fairground. Lostock Hall boxer, Jack McCabe, is in the centre, ready to take on all comers.

This was a scene from Preston's Whitsuntide Fair in June 1946. Judging by the number of raincoats being worn it was clearly an unsettled one for weather.

These women working in the old Town Hall are engaged in preparing the food ration books which the public had to queue for every few months until long after the war was over.

This German Messerschmitt – one of many shot down over Britain in World War Two – was used to promote war savings campaigns. This one with the Nazi swastika shot away on the tail-rudder was sited for a time on the Market Square. Note the brick air-raid shelters on the edge of the square.

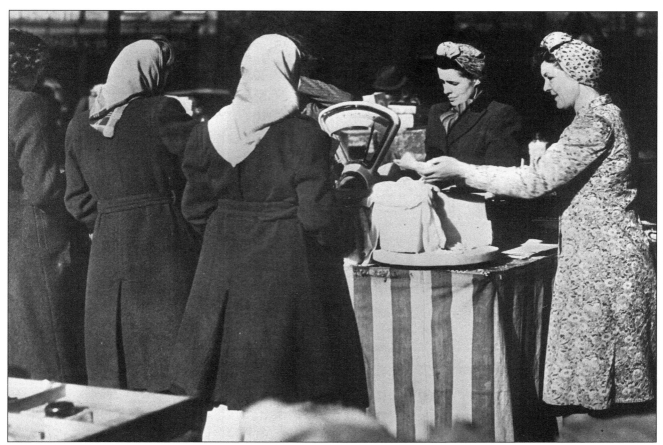

Women in head scarves were a common sight in wartime. These women on Preston covered market are buying the meagre weekly cheese ration.

The *Liseta* petrol tanker after she blew up in Preston Dock in 1943 killing the captain and seven crew. The death toll would have been greater had the other 44 crewmen not gone ashore minutes before. The explosion was an accident and the blast rocked the town.

The Home Guard performed invaluable work during the war. Here they are being inspected on Avenham Park by a high-ranking officer.

The building was used by English Electric Co during the war as a shadow factory in the building of Halifax bombers. Several of these secret factories were scattered throughout the town in case the Strand Road works was bombed. Note the security man at the door and the concrete blocks to obstruct possible invasion tanks. The road direction sign on the right lamp standard would have been removed later. The building is in Fishergate opposite Butler Street.

During the war the Government encouraged 'Stay at Home' holidays. A fairground on Moor Park was one of the features of Preston's 1944 August Holiday Week.

The Home Guard's final parade in Preston on being officially stood down took place in November 1944. Taking the salute is Major-General G. Waterhouse, on his right is Alderman Walter Gordon and on his left is the Mayor, Councillor Gee.

Lancashire Daily Post.

No. 18,166 | REGISTERED AT THE GENERAL POST OFFICE AS A NEWSPAPER | MONDAY, MAY 7, 1945 | Published Daily, 1½d.

IT'S OVER : SURRENDER COMPLETED

ORDER BY DOENITZ TO GERMAN FORCES

GENERALS SIGN AT EISENHOWER'S H.Q.

*T*HE war in Europe is over. The Allies to-day officially announced that Germany had surrendered unconditionally, says a Rheims message.

The surrender took place at 2 41 a.m. (French time) to-day at Gen. Eisenhower's H.Q.

Col.-General Gustav Jodl, the new German Army Chief of Staff, signed for Germany.

General Bedell Smith, Eisenhower's Chief of Staff, signed for the Supreme Allied Command, according to an account of the ceremony broadcast by New York radio.

General Ivan Susoparoff signed for Russia and General Francois Sevez for France.

PREMIER'S PLANS

The "Post" Political Correspondent says the end of the war in Europe will come with the signing of an instrument of surrender by the highest German authorities covering all pockets of resistance in Germany, in France, in Norway, the Channel Islands, and elsewhere.

The Prime Minister's announcement will be short, giving only the main facts. If he is able to give the first flash of the news at the

MEN OF THE HOUR

"Stop" to U-Boats: Cabinet

NAZI TRICKS RIGHT TO THE END

By OUR DIPLOMATIC CORRESPONDENT.

THIS week-end really saw the end of German resistance, but on formal grounds the final surrender of the pitiful remnants of what was once the greatest military power in Europe—in the world perhaps—had to be postponed for a few hours.

The Allies wanted that last act of total submission accomplished in a manner rendering it impossible for the Germans to say later that in their death throes they succeeded in dividing the Big Three.

Norway, therefore, was singled out as a test case: the Western Allies deferred the acceptance of Doenitz's offer to surrender until the Nazi scapegoat agreed to present his surrender simultaneously to the Russians.

Thus VE-Day is upon us. We should not mind Mr. Churchill bottling up that joyful news for a few hours longer. If by so doing it's Allies nip in the bud the enemy's attempt to make a show of surrendering to the Western Powers, while resistance continues to our Russian friends. That sort of typical German intrigue cannot be allowed.

NO LOOPHOLE

Only yesterday the alleged report of a non-existent German High Command headquarters announced that divisions fighting in the West had been transferred to

DEMPSEY IN COPENHAGEN

General Dempsey has arrived in Copenhagen. Kalundborg radio says arrival of Field Marshal Montgomery is expected. — "Post" London Service.

NEW YORK "WILD WITH JOY"

There were wild scenes of joy in New York within few minutes of receipt of Rheims message that Germany had surrendered unconditionally. Ticker tapes and bits of torn-up telephone books started fluttering down from skyscrapers in city's traditional manner of celebration.

LUFTWAFFE HELP R.A.F.

..The Luftwaffe flagged R.A.F. Dakotas into Copenhagen airfield on Saturday afternoon. Shortly afterwards air base and German garrison were formally surrendered to British forces.

WORLD WILL HEAR

The King's broadcast, and Mr. Churchill's on Thursday, will be heard throughout world on a scale never before equalled. Similar measures give fullest facilities in Britain to hear address of President Truman and other Allied leaders.

VICTORY SALVO

London may hear victory salvos on either VE-Day or VE-Day plus

It's over: The *Daily Post* headline says it all. The news that peace-loving people everywhere had long waited for.

As soon as the BBC radio announced on the morning of 8 May 1945, that the Germans had surrendered, people made their way in thousands to the Market Square to share with each other the joyful news.

Apart from the 1939 car models, this scene of Preston North End's West Stand has not changed much. Loxham's Garages Ltd is no longer in existence and neither will this view of West Stand when the present plans to rebuild it materialise around 1996.

A young genius unrecognised. The small boy stood on the engine buffer (centre) in short trousers is 13-year-old Tom Finney, the reserve player with Preston Schoolboys' team in 1936 when they travelled to meet West Ham Boys in the English School's Trophy Final in London. Tom was considered too small to be selected. The match was a draw and the teams shared the trophy.

Tom Finney and his charming bride, Elsie, in 1945 outside Emmanuel Church after their wedding.

Bill Dean, FA Colts trainer, massages Tom Finney's leg before a game at Blackpool watched by George Bromilow (Southport) and Colin Henderson (Heysham), the two linesmen, and Ken Horton (Preston North End).

Tom's farewell – Tom Finney accepts the crowd's applause prior to the kick-off in his final appearance for Preston North End at Deepdale in April 1960, when they beat Luton Town 2-0.

Tom Finney, club president, removes the first turf at Deepdale in 1986 prior to the laying of the controversial plastic pitch which was removed eight years later.

Preston's Famous Ladies. Over the years there have been several Dick, Kerr's Ladies Football teams. Here is the original team which was started in 1917 by women workers at the Preston factory. They began playing to raise money for the Moor Park military hospital during World War One and went on to win world fame for years afterwards.

A group of schoolboy admirers watch Dick, Kerr's Ladies team practise on Moor Park in 1937

Preston Dick, Kerr's FC 1946 team who played Weymouth Ladies FC.

Joan Whalley (holding the ball) discusses tactics with other members of the Dick, Kerr's Ladies Team in the 1946 era.

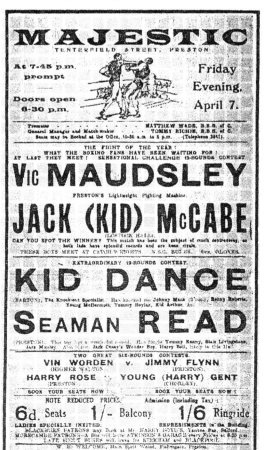

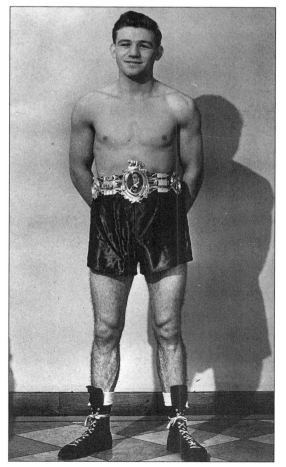

Far left: The majestic in Tenterfield Street, Preston, owned by market trader Matt Wade, was used for boxing, wrestling, roller-skating and dancing. Most of the users of this 1937 bill were local fighters.

Left: Johnny Sullivan, the Preston middleweight, in 1954 when he was the British and Empire champion and a Lonsdale Belt holder.

Hi there, Highness! How about chatting with me down here? Princess Diana in the Children's Ward after she officially opened the Royal Preston Hospital in 1983.

Healing the Sick

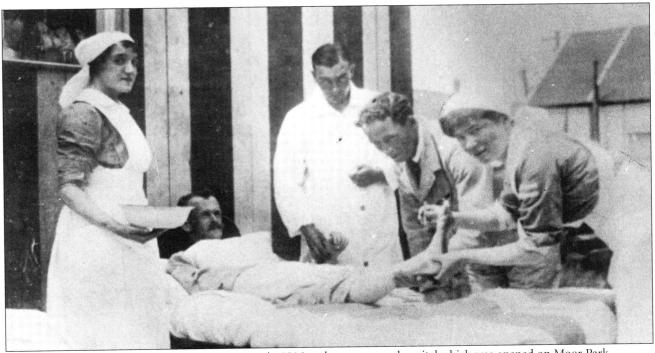

A wounded soldier from France receives treatment in 1916 at the emergency hospital which was opened on Moor Park, Preston.

A skeleton out of the cupboard! This grisly photograph merely shows one of the nurses' training classrooms in use in the thirties at Preston Royal Infirmary.

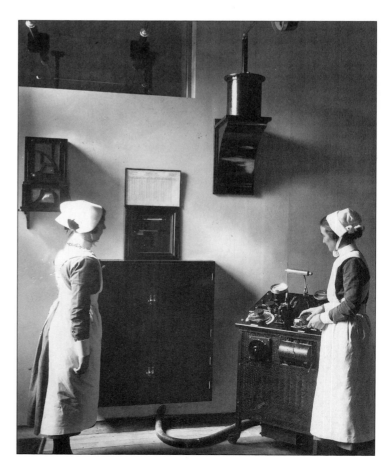

This X-ray machine was the latest technology for treating cancer at Preston Royal Infirmary in 1933.

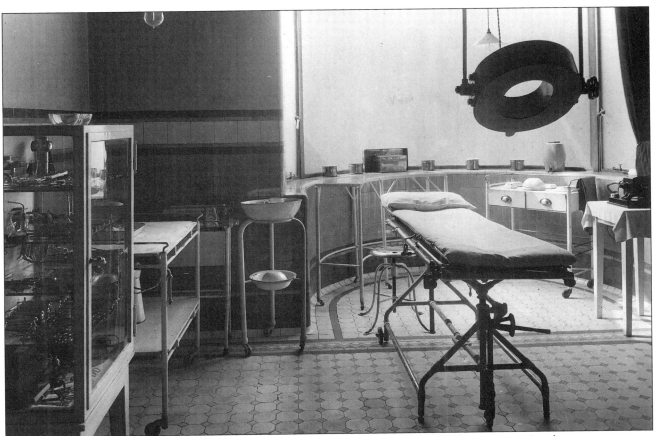

Fluorescent lighting was unheard of in 1936 when this was taken in this Preston Royal Infirmary operating theatre.

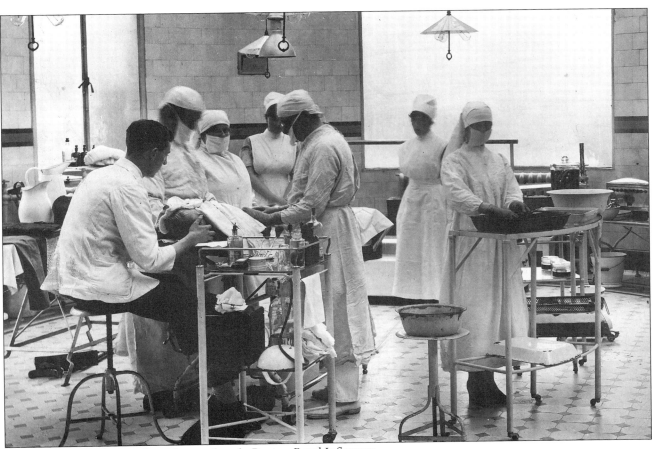

And this was how they performed operations in Preston Royal Infirmary.

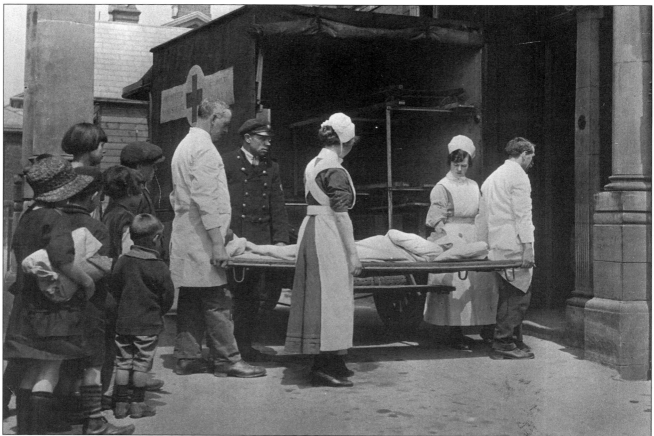

Will he be all right? A heavily bandaged patient is carried into Preston Royal Infirmary in the 1920s, watched by young and sympathetic onlookers. Note the canvas-rolled ambulance exit door.

There was no NHS in existence in 1935 when these out-patients awaited their turn at Preston Royal Infirmary. Casualties were brought into the infirmary by the same entrance and the smell of antiseptics and chloroform was always present.

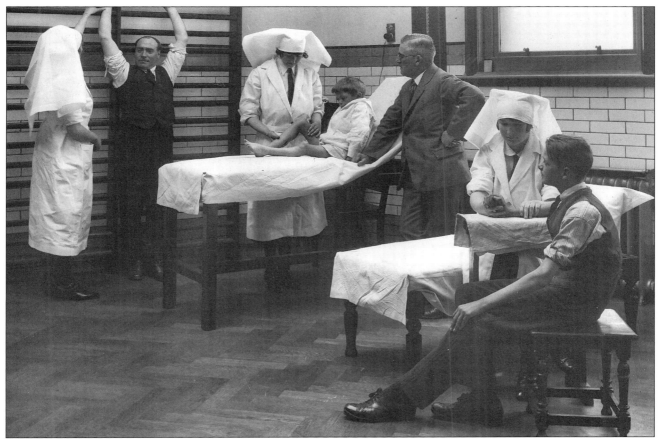

Preston Royal Infirmary patients receiving massage and medical treatment in 1936.

The new maternity wing which was opened at Preston Royal Infirmary in 1936 by the Countess of Derby. The money was raised mainly by voluntary subscriptions.